Ink of Intifada:
Poems for Palestine
Ismael S Rodriguez Jr

Table of Contents

Foreword:

As I hold this anthology in my hands, "Ink of Intifada: Poems for Palestine," I am filled with a profound sense of purpose and passion. Within these pages lies a testament to the resilience, the struggle, and the unwavering spirit of a people longing for justice and freedom.

My name is Ismael, and I stand before you not only as a poet but as an activist, a voice echoing the sentiments of a land yearning to be heard. Each poem contained herein is not merely a collection of words but a fervent plea for recognition, for empathy, for action.

Palestine, a land scarred by history, by conflict, by occupation, has given birth to generations of poets, artists, and activists. Our pens are our swords, our verses our shields, as we navigate the tumultuous landscape of the Palestinian homeland. With every line, we resist. With every stanza, we defy. With every word, we reclaim our narrative.

"Ink of Intifada" is a tribute to the indomitable spirit of the Palestinian people. It is a tapestry woven from the threads of sorrow and hope, of anguish and resilience. Through these poems, you will traverse the winding streets of Gaza, the bustling markets of Ramallah, the serene olive groves of Bethlehem. You will hear the cries of the oppressed, the laughter of children amidst rubble, the whispered prayers for peace.

As the sole poet featured in this anthology, I am humbled to join in solidarity with fellow voices of resistance who have spoken with courage. Together, we illuminate the darkness, we challenge the status quo, we envision a future where justice reigns supreme.

I invite you, dear reader, to immerse yourself in these verses, to let them stir your conscience, to ignite the flames of solidarity within your heart. For Palestine is not merely a distant land on a map; it is a symbol of defiance, of perseverance, of humanity's eternal quest for dignity.

May my poems serve as a beacon of hope in the darkest of times. May they inspire you to stand in solidarity with the oppressed, to speak truth to power, to uphold the values of justice and equality for all.

With ink as our weapon and poetry as our shield, let us continue to write the story of Palestine—one verse at a time.

In solidarity,

Ismael

In the Footsteps of Darwish

In the shadow of an olive tree,
Beneath a sky adorned with memory,
We walk the path Mahmoud Darwish tread,
In the land where dreams and sorrows wed.
In the footsteps of Darwish, we roam,
Through valleys of verse, we find our home,
In every stanza, a tale untold,
Of exile's ache and love's stronghold.
He painted with words the Palestinian plight,
A symphony of longing in the still of the night,
Each line a whisper, each verse a sigh,
Echoes of a land beneath a troubled sky.
From Haifa's shores to Ramallah's hills,
His poetry flowed like mountain rills,
Capturing the essence of a people's pain,
Their hopes, their dreams, their loss, their gain.
In the footsteps of Darwish, we trace,
The yearning for a distant place,
Where orange groves scent the evening air,
And jasmine blooms without a care.
He wrote of home with fervent zeal,
A place where hearts could truly heal,
But exile's chains bound him tight,
To roam the world with restless plight.
In coffeehouses and crowded streets,
His verses danced to rhythmic beats,
Challenging oppression with each word,
In the language of the caged bird.
Oh, how he sang of love's sweet flame,
And the ache of lovers torn by shame,

Yet in his verses, love found a way,
To defy borders, to forever stay.
In the footsteps of Darwish, we find,
A beacon of hope for humankind,
For in his poetry, we see the light,
That guides us through the darkest night.
Though he may have left this earthly sphere,
His spirit lingers, forever near,
In every poem, in every rhyme,
His legacy transcends space and time.
So let us walk in Darwish's wake,
With every word, a stand we take,
For justice, peace, and freedom's call,
In the footsteps of Darwish, we stand tall.

The Night Journey

In the hush of night, a journey unfolds,
Through realms unseen, where tales are told.
A journey of wonder, through heavens high,
Guided by faith, beneath the starry sky.
On wings of dreams, the Prophet soared,
To Jerusalem's gates, where history roared.
Through lands of ancient tales and lore,
Where prophets walked, in times of yore.
Jerusalem, city of eternal flame,
Where hearts converge, regardless of name.
A beacon of hope, a sacred ground,
Where echoes of prayers resound.
In the heart of Palestine, Jerusalem stands,
A symbol of struggle, of resilient hands.
For Palestinians, it's more than just stone,
It's a place they've called home, long known.
The night journey echoes in their plight,
As they yearn for freedom, for their rights.
Through checkpoints and walls, they tread,
With steadfast hearts, and spirits fed.
Their journey, like the Prophet's flight,
Is fueled by faith, in the darkest night.
A longing for justice, a yearning for peace,
In the land where ancient stories cease.
Oh Jerusalem, city of light and grace,
May your walls witness a time and place,
Where all can dwell in harmony's embrace,
And the night journey finds its final trace.

Sons of Abraham

In the ancient sands where tales reside,
A patriarch's footsteps mark the divide.
Abraham, father of faith, revered high,
Binding hearts beneath the same sky.
Sons of Abraham, from varied lands,
Walking paths marked by his guiding hands.
In Palestine's soil, their roots entwine,
Bound by a legacy, divine design.
From Ur's desert to Canaan's plains,
His legacy in every heart remains.
Through Ishmael and Isaac, the lineage flows,
A shared bond that history bestows.
In mosques, synagogues, and churches grand,
Prayers rise, echoing across the land.
The same God worshipped in different ways,
Unites their souls in silent praise.
Yet, amidst the olive groves' whispering leaves,
Echoes of conflict, a sorrow that grieves.
Bound by heritage, yet torn apart,
Brothers in faith with fractured hearts.
In the shadow of ancient walls,
The call for peace softly calls.
Sons of Abraham, let love's light shine,
In the cradle of faith, let harmony align.
For in unity lies the promise unfurled,
Of a land where peace can mend the world.
Sons of Abraham, let hatred cease,
Embrace the heritage of love and peace.

Hagar's Lament

Amidst the sands where whispers die,
    Where the sun scorches the boundless sky,
    Hagar walks with weary feet,
    Her heart heavy, her steps discreet.
    Oh, how the desert wind does wail,
    As Hagar's sorrow tells its tale,
    A mother torn from kin and kin,
    Her tears lost in the dust's cruel spin.
    In exile's grasp, her spirit weeps,
    As memories of home softly creep,
    A distant land, a promised dream,
    Now distant as a distant stream.
    With Ismail by her side, she roams,
    Through deserts vast, through barren zones,
    A bond of love, a bond of pain,
    Their story etched in every grain.
    She calls upon the stars above,
    To guide them with their gentle love,
    But they remain silent, distant, cold,
    As if their hearts were made of mold.
    Oh, Ismail, her precious son,
    Her comfort, her light, her only one,
    Yet even he, in time, will stray,
    Lost to the sands, so far away.
    With trembling hands and aching heart,
    She prays for strength to play her part,
    To endure the trials fate has thrown,
    To find a place they can call home.
    But in the silence of the night,
    She whispers secrets to the light,

Of dreams deferred, of hopes unseen,
Of shattered lives, of what has been.
Hagar's lament echoes wide and far,
A haunting melody beneath the stars,
For every mother who knows the cost,
Of love and loss, of dreams now lost.
In Hagar's voice, we hear the cries,
Of mothers torn 'neath endless skies,
Their pain, their courage, their silent plea,
For justice, peace, and liberty.

Gaza's Canvas: Beauty Amidst the Rubble

In Gaza, where the sun kisses the earth,
And skies of azure echo tales of worth,
A canvas painted with hues so bold,
Yet scars of struggle, stories untold.
Among the rubble, flowers bloom,
In defiance of despair, they resume,
Their petals, whispers of resilience,
Amidst the chaos, a silent brilliance.
The salty breeze whispers ancient lore,
Carrying dreams of peace from shore to shore,
Through narrow alleys, where laughter rings,
And children dance, despite broken strings.
Oh Gaza, cradled by the sea,
Your beauty lies in the eyes that see,
Beyond the walls, beyond the strife,
A testament to the human life.
But shadows linger, where darkness reigns,
And tears mingle with the desert grains,
A landscape scarred by conflict's hand,
Yet hope persists, across the land.
Among the olive trees, stories unfold,
Of hearts steadfast, of spirits bold,
For every ruin, there's a tale to tell,
Of resilience rising, breaking the spell.
Gaza, your spirit knows no bounds,
In your resilience, humanity resounds,
A masterpiece amidst the stormy night,
Guiding us towards the morning light.

So let us paint a picture true,
Of Gaza's beauty, of skies so blue,
And in our hearts, let solidarity rise,
As we stand with Gaza, under the same skies.

Voices of the Prophet

In the heart of ancient sands, where prophets roamed,
Their voices echo through time, like whispered poems.
Moses, with staff in hand, parted the sea,
Leading his people to freedom, setting them free.
Jesus, the healer, with love in his eyes,
Preached of compassion, under azure skies.
Muhammad, the last, with the Quran's light,
Guided his followers through darkest night.
Their words, like threads woven into the land,
Binding together the faithful, hand in hand.
In Palestine's soil, where olives still grow,
Their teachings linger, a steadfast glow.
"Justice," they cry, from ages past,
Injustice shatters, like brittle glass.
"Compassion," they whisper, in every breeze,
Softening hearts, bringing souls to ease.
"Solidarity," they call, across the divide,
Uniting humanity, side by side.
In the struggle of Palestine, their voices ring clear,
Echoing hope, dispelling fear.
For in the legacy of prophets, we find,
The strength to resist, the courage to bind.
In their timeless words, we stand tall,
Voices of the prophet, echoing for all.

Divine Displacement

In sacred scrolls, the tales unfold,
Of lands revered, of stories old.
Where prophets roamed and miracles rose,
In timeless whispers, the truth exposed.
Jerusalem, where heavens descend,
A city of faith, where prayers transcend.
Yet in its streets, echoes resound,
Of a people displaced, their cries unbound.
Divine displacement, a paradox profound,
Where holy ground meets earthly mound.
The soil soaked in history's tears,
Bearing witness to hopes and fears.
In Bethlehem's cradle, a babe was born,
Yet Bethlehem's children are left forlorn.
Their homes uprooted, their orchards razed,
By forces that see but fail to gaze.
Mountains of Zion, where songs ascend,
Yet in its shadows, lives suspend.
For every psalm that fills the air,
There's a lament for what's no longer there.
From Hebron's hills to Gaza's shore,
The stories echo evermore.
Of ancient ties and modern plight,
Of faith tested in the darkest night.
But amid the rubble, resilience thrives,
In steadfast hearts, hope survives.
For the spirit knows no bounds or walls,
It rises above, it heeds the calls.
Divine displacement, a burden borne,
Yet in the ashes, seeds are sown.

For from the dust, new life will rise,
In the land where the divine still lies.

The Conquest of Mecca

In the dawn's gentle hue, where shadows fade,
A tale of conquest, yet no sword was swayed.
Mecca's sacred sands, where faith had stood,
Now witnessed peace, where once blood had flowed.
Through valleys deep and mountains tall,
The Prophet led, with compassion's call.
Not with steel, nor with wrathful cry,
But with love's embrace, beneath the sky.
In hearts once hardened by years of strife,
A seed of mercy, a spark of life.
Forgiveness blossomed, like desert bloom,
Swept away the gloom, dispelled the gloom.
As banners waved in the breeze's dance,
Echoes of peace, a new romance.
For in the conquest of Mecca's gate,
Lies a lesson profound, for every state.
That justice's song, sung without sword,
Can pierce the silence, be widely heard.
And reconciliation's gentle hand,
Can mend the tears in the fabric of the land.
So let us heed this ancient tale,
Of how forgiveness can never fail.
For in the conquest of Mecca's reign,
Lies the power of love, forever to sustain.

Bridges of Solidarity

In the echoes of history's tapestry,
Where threads of struggle weave,
Latinos and Palestinians find
Their stories intertwined, believe.
Across distant lands and seas,
Beneath the same sky's grace,
Hands clasped in solidarity,
Hearts beating in one embrace.
In the heat of relentless suns,
Where oppression casts its shadow,
They stand together, side by side,
Against the currents of sorrow.
In the streets where voices rise,
In chants that echo loud and clear,
They march as one, undeterred,
In defiance of all fear.
In the rhythm of ancient drums,
In the dance of resistance bold,
They find strength in unity,
In the stories yet untold.
Through the trials and tribulations,
Through the pain that scars the soul,
They share burdens, shoulder to shoulder,
Seeking justice, striving for the whole.
In the embrace of solidarity,
They find the power to rise,
To break the chains of injustice,
To reach for freedom's skies.
For in the union of hearts and minds,
In the bonds that hold them tight,

They build bridges of hope and peace,
Illuminating the darkest night.
So let the world bear witness,
To this alliance strong and true,
For in solidarity's embrace,
Lies the promise of a brighter hue.

Echoes in the Café

In the heart of a bustling Palestinian café,
    Where the aroma of coffee dances in the air,
    Amidst the clinking of cups and saucers,
    And the melody of laughter everywhere.
    Here, voices rise like the morning sun,
    Each one a thread in the tapestry of the day,
    Telling tales of joy, sorrow, and hope,
    In this sanctuary where souls find their way.
    The walls, adorned with echoes of the past,
    Whisper secrets of resistance and pride,
    As memories linger in the smoky haze,
    And the spirit of resilience cannot hide.
    In corners, old friends gather 'round,
    Sharing stories of struggles overcome,
    Their laughter, a beacon of defiance,
    Against the darkness, they won't succumb.
    Amidst the chatter and clatter of life,
    Echoes of resistance ring clear and true,
    For in this café, it's more than just coffee,
    It's a symbol of strength, a lifeline anew.
    So let the world outside rage on,
    In here, hope's flame will always burn bright,
    In the heart of this Palestinian café,
    Where echoes of resistance take flight.

Sacred Soil, Sacred Tears

In the shadow of ancient stones, we weep,
Where olive groves whisper secrets deep.
Jerusalem's heart, a tapestry of tears,
Holds memories of joy, now shrouded in fears.
Sacred sites echo with prayers unheard,
As history's whispers mingle with every word.
The dome's golden hue, a beacon of hope,
But shadows linger where dreams elope.
Families torn from ancestral lands,
Their cries echo across desert sands.
Roots intertwined with the soil's embrace,
Now severed by conflict, leaving empty space.
In the silence of twilight, ghosts roam,
Through streets where memories once found home.
The laughter of children, a distant refrain,
Lost amid rubble, sorrow, and pain.
Yet in the midst of this turmoil and plight,
Flames of resilience burn ever bright.
For every tear shed, a seed is sown,
In the soil of resistance, courage is grown.
In the face of adversity, we stand tall,
United in purpose, we heed the call.
For justice, for peace, our voices rise,
Echoing beneath Palestine's azure skies.
Though scars may mar the landscape's face,
Hope blooms anew in this sacred space.
For the spirit of Palestine, unyielding and true,
Shall endure, rise, and triumph anew.

Silent Cries, Endless Skies

In lands where olive branches weep,
> Underneath the sun's relentless sweep,
> A tale of sorrow, a story so deep,
> End the occupation, let justice seep.
> In Palestine's heart, where shadows loom,
> Amidst the dust, amid the gloom,
> A longing for freedom, a silent fume,
> End the occupation, let hope resume.
> From ancient streets to modern plight,
> Where children dream beneath starry light,
> Their laughter muffled, out of sight,
> End the occupation, let their futures ignite.
> Amidst the rubble, amidst the cries,
> Where mothers weep under tear-streaked skies,
> Their prayers ascend, a plea that flies,
> End the occupation, let truth arise.
> In the cradle of history, where echoes reside,
> Where dreams of peace refuse to hide,
> A call resounds, far and wide,
> End the occupation, let humanity's tide.
> For every soul yearning to be free,
> For every heart longing to see,
> A land where justice reigns, where all can be,
> End the occupation, let Palestine breathe.

In the Shadow of Olive Trees

In the shadow of olive trees, they stand,
A land of stories, etched in sand.
Palestinian souls, resilient, true,
Beneath the sky, where dreams pursue.
In ancient groves, whispers linger,
Echoes of struggle, fingers point to the finger,
Each tree a witness, each branch a tale,
Of resilience, of hope, in the gale.
Through tumult, through the darkest nights,
Underneath the crescent moon's soft light,
They weave their dreams, they hold their ground,
In the shadow where hope is found.
In Gaza's streets, where tears flow free,
And whispers rise to plea and decree,
Amongst the ruins, amidst the strife,
They carve their path, reclaiming life.
From Ramallah to Jerusalem's call,
Their voices rise, they stand tall,
In the heart of Hebron, where echoes dwell,
Their story unfolds, a tale to tell.
In the shadow of olive trees, they fight,
For dignity, for freedom, in the night.
Their struggle echoes through the land,
A testament to courage, hand in hand.
In the face of oppression, they stand bold,
Their story written, never to be sold.
In the shadow of olive trees, they rise,
In the Palestinian struggle, their spirits fly.

Caffeine Chronicles

In the heart of Palestine's ancient land,
　　Where olive groves stretch by golden sand,
　　Lies a tapestry woven with threads of strife,
　　Yet amidst the chaos, a rhythm of life.
　　In Ramallah's bustling streets, at dawn's first light,
　　Where the muezzin's call mingles with birds in flight,
　　Old men gather 'neath the shade of fig trees,
　　Sipping dark coffee, telling tales with ease.
　　Their wrinkled hands cradle cups worn and chipped,
　　As they reminisce of the past, never eclipsed,
　　By the hardships endured, the struggles faced,
　　Coffee's warmth a balm in this sacred space.
　　In Gaza's narrow alleys, where children play,
　　Amidst rubble and ruins, hope finds its way,
　　Mothers brew cardamom-spiced coffee, strong,
　　Serving strength with each cup, all day long.
　　Their laughter dances amidst the chaos and pain,
　　Coffee's aroma weaving joy through the strain,
　　For in each bitter sip, they find a taste,
　　Of resilience, of courage, in this tumultuous place.
　　In Bethlehem's ancient squares, where tourists roam,
　　Amidst centuries-old stones, a sense of home,
　　Artist's sketch scenes of daily life, alive,
　　Capturing moments where coffee thrives.
　　In each stroke of the brush, each line that's drawn,
　　Coffee's presence lingers from dusk 'til dawn,
　　A symbol of unity, of culture, of pride,
　　In these caffeine chronicles, where stories abide.
　　From Jenin's olive groves to Hebron's ancient walls,
　　Coffee's journey echoes through bustling stalls,

A thread that binds the past to the present day,
In Palestine's story, it finds its way.
So let us raise our cups, filled with memories dear,
To the land of Palestine, where hope is near,
In these caffeine chronicles, may we find,
Strength in unity, and peace for all time.

Palestine's Resolve

In lands where sun kisses the sand,
Palestine stands, a storied land,
Beneath the gaze of ancient skies,
Where echoes of resolve arise.
Through olive groves, the whispers roam,
In every heart, a cherished home,
With every dawn, a steadfast vow,
To rise, to fight, to claim their now.
In Gaza's streets, where tears may flow,
They plant the seeds that courage sow,
With steadfast hearts, they face the night,
In Palestine, the spirit's light.
From Bethlehem's manger to Gaza's shore,
Their voices rise, their cries implore,
For justice, peace, and liberty,
In Palestine's unwavering plea.
Though walls may rise, and borders stand,
Their dreams like stars, forever grand,
In every child's unwavering eyes,
Palestine's resolve, it never dies.
Through trials faced, through trials yet to come,
Their spirit soars, their beat drums,
In every heartbeat, freedom's call,
Palestine stands, unyielding, tall.
So let the world, with open ear,
Hear Palestine's resolve, so clear,
For in their fight, their truth, their song,
Palestine's resilience, forever strong.

In the Sands of Time

In the sands of time, where echoes wail,
Palestine's story, an ancient tale,
Amidst the dunes, where memories gleam,
Lies the heart of a people, a steadfast dream.
Beneath the sun, by olive's shade,
Their struggle etched, their courage displayed,
In the whispering winds, their voices rise,
Resilience woven beneath desert skies.
From Gaza's shores to Ramallah's call,
They stand united, they never fall,
In the face of darkness, they seek the light,
Guided by justice, fueled by the fight.
In the sands of time, where empires fade,
Palestine's spirit, never swayed,
Through conquests fierce and occupations grim,
They hold onto hope, their vision within.
Through tears that fall like morning dew,
Their dreams persist, their strength renew,
For every stone thrown, for every cry,
Their truth resounds, refusing to die.
In the shadows cast by ancient walls,
Their resilience stands, as history recalls,
In the whispers of ancestors, they find their song,
A melody of freedom, enduring and strong.
In the sands of time, their story told,
A tale of courage, of hearts bold,
For Palestine's struggle, everlasting and true,
In the sands of time, their spirit imbued.

Olive Branches and Barbed Wire

In the land where ancient olive trees sway,
Their branches whisper secrets of yesteryears,
Roots entwined with tales of resilience,
In Palestinian soil, amid joys and tears.
Olive trees, guardians of the land,
Symbolize peace, rooted deep in history,
Their branches extend like outstretched hands,
Embracing hope in the face of adversity.
But in the shadow of looming walls,
Barbed wire coils, dividing hearts asunder,
Each strand a symbol of oppression's call,
Yet, amidst the darkness, resilience does not falter.
For every branch that bears the weight of sorrow,
Every leaf that trembles with the winds of strife,
There's a spirit that refuses to bow,
A testament to the endurance of Palestinian life.
Olive groves witness the dance of generations,
Their gnarled trunks stand as monuments to time,
Bearing witness to struggles and aspirations,
Inscribed in the lines of their age-old rhyme.
Despite the wounds inflicted by conflict's ire,
Olive branches still reach for the azure sky,
Symbolizing hope that will never tire,
An unwavering call for justice, flying high.
So let the world heed the tale they tell,
Of olive branches and barbed wire's sting,
In the heart of Palestine, where dreams dwell,
Hope blooms eternal, as the olive trees sing.

Steaming Cups and Solidarity

In the heart of bustling streets, where shadows dance with light,
Amidst the echoes of unrest, in the stillness of the night,
There brews a potent potion, in cups both old and worn,
A blend of bitter solace, a taste of hope reborn.
Steaming cups and solidarity, in each sip, a shared refrain,
In the swirls of rising steam, a bond that will remain.
For in the humble coffee grounds, lies a tale untold,
Of resilience and unity, in the stories that unfold.
With calloused hands, they gather, seekers of reprieve,
In the warmth of camaraderie, their burdens they relieve.
Each sip a silent pledge, to stand in unity's embrace,
To weather storms together, in this sacred, shared space.
Through the haze of uncertainty, they find a common thread,
In the aroma of tradition, in the words that go unsaid.
For in the simple act of sharing, lies a strength profound,
A resilience in solidarity, in every cup, it's found.
In the rhythm of their breathing, in the whispers of their sighs,
They find the courage to endure, beneath tumultuous skies.
For when the world seems fractured, and hope begins to wane,
Steaming cups and solidarity, kindle the flame again.
So let the coffee brew anew, let its fragrance fill the air,
For in the midst of strife and struggle, solidarity stands fair.
In the warmth of shared compassion, in the depths of human grace,
Steaming cups and solidarity illuminate the darkest place.

Seeds of Hope

In the midst of rubble and despair,
  Amidst the echoes of strife in the air,
  We plant the seeds of hope, so fair,
  In the soil of our land, burdened yet aware.
  Beneath the weight of occupation's might,
  Where darkness shrouds both day and night,
  Our hands embrace the soil, holding tight,
  Nurturing dreams of freedom's light.
  Each seed we sow, a silent vow,
  To defy oppression, to break the plow
  Of injustice, and to fervently avow,
  That our roots run deep, our spirits endow.
  Through tears that mingle with the rain,
  And whispers that echo through the grain,
  We tend to the seeds, despite the pain,
  Believing in a future where we'll regain.
  For every seed holds a promise true,
  Of a land where skies are forever blue,
  Where laughter dances, where dreams renew,
  And where peace and prosperity breakthrough.
  Though storms may rage, and winds may blow,
  And though the path ahead may seem slow,
  The seeds of hope within us grow,
  Fueling our spirits, aglow.
  And as we tend to each tender shoot,
  We envision a land where justice takes root,
  Where every voice, in harmony, will flute,
  In a symphony of freedom, resolute.
  So, amidst the rubble, amidst the strife,
  We plant the seeds, for our shared life,

Nurturing dreams amidst the strife,
For a future of peace, beyond the knife.
With every sunrise, with every dawn,
The seeds of hope endure and spawn,
A testament to the spirit drawn,
From the soil of our land, forever reborn.

The Keys of Return

In the palm of every refugee's hand,
    Lies a key, heavy with memory,
    Each one a silent witness, a steadfast stand,
    A symbol of a longing that won't flee.
    These keys of return, weathered and worn,
    Unveil tales of displacement and yearning,
    They whisper of the land where they were born,
    And the flames of hope, ceaselessly burning.
    Carried across borders, over deserts wide,
    Through generations, they pass with care,
    With every step, they silently confide,
    A legacy of resilience, too heavy to bear.
    In the heart of each key lies a home,
    A sanctuary lost, yet never forgotten,
    Where ancient olive trees freely roam,
    And dreams of return are softly begotten.
    They speak of villages nestled in the hills,
    Where laughter once echoed in the air,
    Of bustling markets and ancient mills,
    And the fragrance of jasmine, beyond compare.
    With every turn of the key, a prayer ascends,
    For the day when walls and barriers will fall,
    When hearts and homes, broken, will mend,
    And the echo of freedom will answer the call.
    So let the keys of return forever remind,
    Of a people's unwavering commitment to stand,
    In the face of injustice, they steadfastly find,
    Their home, their heritage, reclaimed by their hand.

In the Shadow of Walls

In the shadow of walls, where sunlight fades,
Palestinian families endure beneath oppressive shades.
Barriers rise, dividing hearts and lands,
Yet their spirit remains unbroken, their unity stands.
Checkpoints loom like sentinels of despair,
Separating kin, shattering dreams with cold air.
But in the midst of this relentless siege,
Love's flame persists, refusing to submerge.
Mothers clutch their children with steadfast grace,
Their embrace a fortress in this desolate space.
Fathers teach resilience with each whispered word,
In the face of adversity, their voices are heard.
Through the cracks of concrete, hope still gleams,
In the depths of darkness, faith redeems.
For in the hearts of Palestinian families, resilient and bold,
Lies the strength to defy, the spirit to uphold.
They weave threads of connection, despite the divide,
A tapestry of love that cannot be denied.
In the shadow of walls, they find a way,
To bridge the chasm, to greet the light of day.
Their laughter echoes defiance, their tears a testament,
To the human spirit, unyielding and fervent.
For in the shadow of walls, where barriers stand tall,
Palestinian families rise, unbroken by the fall.
Their story is one of courage, their journey, sublime,
In the face of oppression, they endure, they climb.
For love knows no borders, no walls can contain,
The resilience of families who dare to remain.
In the shadow of walls, they stand as one,
Bound by love, under the same sun.

Their spirit unyielding, their resolve ever strong,
In the face of injustice, they sing freedom's song.

The Dance of Survival

In the land where olives weep,
Palestinian families sway and leap,
Amidst the shadows of walls so steep,
In the dance of survival, they find their keep.
Beneath the weight of occupation's yoke,
They rise with every breath they invoke,
Their steps echo defiance, their spirits bespoke,
In the rhythm of resistance, they provoke.
With every beat, they defy despair,
Their movements tell tales of a people's prayer,
Through hardship and anguish, they declare,
Love, laughter, and solidarity, their solitaire.
In the midst of turmoil, they find their grace,
Gathered in homes, in a tight embrace,
Their laughter echoes in defiance of the chase,
As they weave through hardship with unwavering pace.
Their bodies sway like the olive trees,
Rooted deep in the soil, they refuse to appease,
For love knows no bounds, as it tirelessly frees,
In the dance of survival, they find their peace.
Together they stand, hand in hand,
In the face of oppression, they make their stand,
Their resilience a beacon across the land,
As they dance through the darkness, hand in hand.
In the rhythm of survival, they find their voice,
In the dance of resistance, they rejoice,
For love, laughter, and solidarity, their choice,
Guiding them through the night, with unwavering poise.
So let the world witness their unwavering drive,
As they dance through the chaos, they truly thrive,

For in their unity, they shall forever strive,
In the dance of survival, they come alive.

Echoes of Loss and Longing

In Gaza's streets, where shadows weep,
Palestinian orphans softly tread,
Their tiny hearts, in sorrow steep,
With memories of the homes they fled.
Lost in the tumult of endless strife,
Their families torn by war's cruel hand,
They carry burdens, carved by life,
In a broken, unforgiving land.
Their eyes, a mirror of distant shores,
Reflect the stars of ancestral skies,
As they dream of open doors,
Where peace's gentle whispers rise.
Oh, how they long for a mother's embrace,
Amidst the chaos, the gunfire's roar,
Seeking solace in a sacred place,
Where love's warmth, they knew before.
They wander through the rubble's maze,
Amidst the ruins, they softly cry,
In search of lost, forgotten days,
Beneath the Palestinian sky.
Their tears, like rivers, flow unseen,
A silent stream of anguish deep,
As they cling to memories, evergreen,
In the silence of the night's weep.
Yet still, they carry hope's bright flame,
A beacon in the darkest night,
Believing in a world untamed,
Where justice blooms, in morning light.
For in their hearts, a song remains,
A testament to resilience strong,

A melody of courage that sustains,
In the echo of loss and longing's song.
So let us hear their voices rise,
In solidarity, hand in hand,
As we vow to dry their tear-stained eyes,
And rebuild their shattered land.

Echoes of Legacy: Palestinian Resilience

In the shadow of olive groves, where echoes linger long,
A legacy of generations, a timeless, ancient song.
Palestinian soil, rich with tales, whispers stories untold,
Of resilience forged in hardship, of courage manifold.
From elders' lips to children's ears, the stories gently flow,
Of lands lost, and dreams shattered, of wounds that still bestow.
Through the tumult of the ages, through trials and through tears,
Runs a thread of steadfast spirit, through the passing years.
The legacy of generations, etched in every stone,
In every heart that beats with pride, in every child alone.
For in the face of adversity, they find the strength to stand,
To uphold the honor of their kin, to reclaim their stolen land.
Palestinian orphans, heirs to a legacy profound,
Carry forth the flame of hope, where hope once seemed unbound.
In their eyes, the fire of their ancestors burns bright,
Igniting dreams of freedom, in the darkest of the night.
Though the winds of injustice howl, and storms may rage and roar,
The legacy of generations shines evermore.
For in the hearts of Palestine, resilience finds its home,
And through the trials of history, its spirit still will roam.
So let us honor the legacy, let us heed its call,
To stand in solidarity, to rise and never fall.
For in the echoes of our past, we find the strength to fight,
To build a future worthy of our legacy's light.

In the Shadow of Olive Trees

In lands where olive trees stand tall,
Amidst the cries, the ancient call,
Palestine, a land of strife,
Where shadows dance in the night's life.
Through olive groves and dusty streets,
Where history and pain discreet,
The people rise, their voices swell,
In the fight for Palestine, they dwell.
A land of prophets, tales untold,
With memories etched in sands of old,
They fight like hell, against the odds,
For freedom's breath, against the gods.
In Gaza's streets, where children weep,
And mothers hold their dreams to keep,
They stand as one, with hearts aflame,
To reclaim dignity, to heal the blame.
From Jenin's alleys to Bethlehem's morn,
Their resilience, a crown proudly worn,
With every stone, with every prayer,
They defy the oppressor's snare.
In refugee camps, beneath the sky,
Their spirit soars, they never die,
For Palestine, they raise the cry,
A fervent anthem, reaching high.
Through tear gas clouds and barricades,
They march, they sing, in serenades,
Their homeland's name upon their tongue,
In the fight, they stand, forever young.
Though the struggle may seem long and steep,
Their courage, a flame they vigilantly keep,

For justice, they rise, they will not rest,
In the fight for Palestine, they are blessed.
So let the world hear their fervent call,
As they rise, they stand, they never fall,
In the echoes of history's knell,
They fight like hell for Palestine, they dwell.

Echoes of Nakba

In the shadows of history's relentless march,
Lies a tale of anguish, a nation's wrenching arch,
Echoes of Nakba, a solemn refrain,
In the hearts of Palestinians, eternally stained.
From the land of olive groves, a cry arose,
As the sun set on homes, where memories froze,
In '48, the winds of fate blew cruel and cold,
Displacing lives, stories untold.
The Nakba, a cataclysmic rupture of soul,
Tore through the fabric, leaving sorrow as its toll,
Homesteads abandoned, orchards left to wither,
As the land wept, under oppression's slither.
The key to homes, a symbol of yearning's plight,
Clutched by generations, through the darkest night,
In exile's embrace, dreams lingered on,
Of return to ancestral soil, where hope had once dawned.
In refugee camps, resilience found its voice,
Echoing defiance, against forces devoid of choice,
The diaspora scattered, yet the spirit endured,
In the face of injustice, unwavering, unperturbed.
From Gaza's shores to Jerusalem's ancient walls,
The heartbeat of a nation, steadfastly calls,
For justice to unfurl its righteous wings,
And redemption to echo, as the morning sings.
The olive tree stands, a testament to resilience,
Rooted deep in the earth, defying all silence,
Its branches reaching, towards a sky so vast,
A metaphor for endurance, steadfast to the last.
Oh, Echoes of Nakba, resounding through time,
In the tapestry of struggle, a narrative sublime,

For the longing for homeland, burns bright and true,
In the hearts of Palestinians, in every hue.
So let the world hear, let justice prevail,
Let peace be the anthem, that will never fail,
For in the echoes of Nakba, lies a story untold,
Of a people's resilience, in the face of the cold.

Ode to Palestine's Mothers

O, mothers of Palestine, hear our ode,
In your strength, a story profoundly sewed,
Amidst the tumult, your courage stands tall,
Guardians of hope, in times of the thrall.
In the cradle of conflict, you gently sway,
Nurturing dreams as dusk meets the day,
Your embrace, a haven in the storm's might,
Guiding your children through the darkest night.
Through tear-streaked skies and sorrow's embrace,
You carry the burdens with unwavering grace,
Your whispers of love, a soothing balm,
Amidst the chaos, a tranquil calm.
In the shadow of walls, where shadows loom,
Your resilience blooms, dispelling the gloom,
With every heartbeat, with every breath,
You kindle the flames of life, even in death.
O, mothers of Palestine, your tears may flow,
Yet within each drop, a seed of hope you sow,
For in your embrace, futures take flight,
A testament to love's enduring might.
In your eyes, the stories of generations past,
Of struggles endured, of memories that last,
Through trials and triumphs, you stand as one,
In the heart of Palestine, beneath the sun.
O, mothers of Palestine, your strength, a song,
Resounding through valleys, where echoes belong,
In your love, a beacon, forever bright,
Guiding us through the darkest night.

Silent Screams of Gaza

In Gaza's heart, where shadows lie deep,
Whispers of anguish, silent screams seep,
Through streets adorned with echoes of woe,
Where sorrow's veil casts a somber glow.
Beneath the weight of relentless siege,
Innocent lives caught in history's siege,
Children's laughter drowned in the night,
In the shattered silence, dreams take flight.
The world turns away, deaf to their plea,
As Gaza's tears merge with the endless sea,
Yet within each soul, a flame still burns bright,
Defiance against the darkest of night.
In the rubble, resilience stands tall,
In the face of oppression, they rise, they call,
For justice, for peace, for a land to be free,
Gaza's spirit, a beacon for all to see.
Though silenced by walls of indifference and pain,
Their voices echo, a haunting refrain,
In the silent screams of Gaza's despair,
A plea for humanity, a hope in the air.
May their cries be heard across lands and seas,
May hearts awaken to their silent pleas,
For in Gaza's quiet, resilience thrives,
A testament to the human spirit that survives.

Whispers of Freedom

In the shadows of ancient stones,
    Where tales of resilience are etched in bone,
    Amidst the olive groves' whispered plea,
    I hear the echoes of a people's decree.
    In the hush of the evening breeze,
    A chorus of dreams, soft melodies,
    Where the stars above silently gleam,
    I glimpse the hope of a longed-for dream.
    Through the darkness of a troubled night,
    Where tears mingle with the fading light,
    There's a flicker, a spark, a gentle flame,
    Igniting hearts with an unwavering aim.
    For in the heart of every child's eyes,
    Lies the promise of sun-kissed skies,
    In every elder's weathered hand,
    Resides the strength to reclaim their land.
    Though walls may rise, and barriers stand tall,
    And injustice weaves its bitter thrall,
    In the whispers of freedom, we find our might,
    Guiding us through the darkest night.
    With every step, with every stride,
    We march together, side by side,
    Towards the dawn of a new day,
    Where justice reigns, and freedom holds sway.
    So let the whispers of freedom grow,
    Into a chorus that all shall know,
    For in the depths of our shared plight,
    Lies the seed of a future bright.
    O Palestine, hear our call,
    Your liberation, our eternal goal,

In the whispers of freedom, we unite,
Until justice prevails, and freedom takes flight.

Eternal Exodus

In sands of time where history's tales are told,
Two peoples' destinies in parallel unfold.
One, an ancient saga of a journey grand,
The other, a modern struggle for their land.
From Egypt's grasp, the Israelites did flee,
Through parted waves, they sought to be free.
Their exodus, a quest for promised shores,
A liberation hymn that echoes evermore.
Yet in the shadow of those parted seas,
Another people yearn for their release.
Palestinians, bound by walls and strife,
Long for the freedom to reclaim their life.
Like Moses' plea to Pharaoh's throne,
Their cries for justice ring, but not alone.
For in the heart of every refugee's lament,
Resounds the echo of a sacred testament.
Two exoduses entwined in fate's embrace,
A timeless struggle for a resting place.
The Israelites, once wanderers in the night,
Now hold the keys to another's plight.
Yet in this saga, hope is not undone,
For in every setting of the setting sun,
Lies the promise of a homeland yet to be,
Where both may dwell in peace and harmony.
So let us heed the lessons of the past,
And build a future where freedom lasts.
Where every soul, regardless of their creed,
May find the refuge they so desperately need.
In this eternal exodus, may we find,
The common bonds that unite mankind.

For in the longing for a place to call our own,
Lies the shared dream that we are not alone.

Children of Stones

In streets of dust and twilight's hue,
    Where echoes of unrest ensue,
    There walk the children, brave and bold,
    Their innocence, a tale untold.
    With stones in hand, their hearts alight,
    They stand against the dark of night,
    Their tiny frames, their voices rise,
    Defiant 'neath the troubled skies.
    In their eyes, a flicker bright,
    Reflecting stars, though dim in plight,
    Each stone a symbol, cast in rage,
    Yet innocence, their tender stage.
    No games of youth, no laughter's ring,
    In shadows where the echoes sing,
    But still they stand, against the wrongs,
    Their cries a protest, pure and strong.
    Oh, children of stones, your burden great,
    Yet in your hearts, a flame innate,
    For in each throw, defiance shown,
    In every step, a courage known.
    Though innocence may fade away,
    In this tumultuous ballet,
    Your bravery shines, a beacon clear,
    A testament to hope sincere.
    In streets of dust, where shadows loom,
    You are the flowers in the gloom,
    Children of stones, in protest bold,
    Your story's tale forever told.

The Prophet's Call

In the hush of the desert's whispered breeze,
A call echoed forth, across land and seas.
A prophet arose with a message divine,
Of justice, compassion, a radiant sign.
From humble beginnings, his voice did ring,
Through valleys and mountains, it soared on the wing.
He spoke of equality, for rich and for poor,
A beacon of light in a world unsure.
In the heart of his message, a steadfast decree,
To stand for the oppressed, to set them free.
With words as his weapons, he battled the wrong,
Guiding his people to where they belong.
His call was not silent, his mission not small,
To champion the downtrodden, to answer their call.
In the face of injustice, he stood undeterred,
A voice for the voiceless, his message assured.
And now, in the land where the olive trees weep,
Where walls stand as barriers, vigil they keep.
The echo of his call still resonates clear,
Inspiring the oppressed, dispelling their fear.
For in the struggle of Palestine's fight,
His teachings illuminate the darkest night.
A legacy of compassion, a beacon so bright,
Guiding the way to justice's height.
So, heed now the call, let its message ignite,
In the hearts of the weary, the oppressed in their plight.
For in justice and compassion, we shall find our way,
United in purpose, until the dawn of that day.

Solidarity's Resolve

In the cradle of ancient lands, where olive trees whisper tales,
Lies a place besieged by injustice, where justice often fails.
Gaza, adorned with the hues of suffering, its skies heavy with plight,
A land where dreams are shattered, where darkness conquers light.
In the shadow of towering walls, where hopes are barred and bound,
Palestinian voices echo, a symphony of resilience resound.
They stand amidst the rubble, amid the cries of sorrow,
Their spirits unbowed, their courage they borrow.
Injustice, a relentless tempest, sweeps across the Gaza sands,
Leaving broken lives and shattered dreams in its demanding hands.
Children orphaned by conflict, mothers mourning their slain,
In the heart of this tragedy, humanity's cries remain.
Solidarity, a beacon in the night, a flame that never wanes,
A chorus of voices rising, breaking through oppression's chains.
From every corner of the earth, hearts beat as one,
In solidarity, our strength, our battle cry begun.
We condemn the injustice, the violations, the pain,
We stand with Palestine, our voices like thunderous rain.
For every life lost, for every dream deferred,
In the face of tyranny, our solidarity is conferred.
The olive branch, a symbol of peace, of hope in despair,
In Gaza's soil, it thrives, a testament to resilience rare.
Let it be known across the ages, let history record our plea,
That justice shall prevail, and Palestine shall be free.
From the river to the sea, from the mountains to the shore,
Palestinian voices echo, demanding freedom evermore.
Injustice shall crumble, solidarity shall reign,
And in Gaza's embrace, humanity shall reclaim.

So let us stand together, in solidarity strong and true,
For the cause of Palestine, for justice overdue.
In the face of oppression, in the depths of despair,
Solidarity's light shines bright, a promise in the air.
May the echoes of resilience resound across the land,
Until Palestine stands tall, until justice takes its stand.
Injustice shall falter, solidarity shall prevail,
And in the heart of Gaza, freedom's song shall never fail.

Echoes of Suffering: The Siege of Gaza

In Gaza's heart, where dreams collide,
Beneath the sun, where hopes abide,
Lies a land besieged, a people tried,
In shadows cast by tears they've cried.
The siege of Gaza, a tale untold,
Where stories whisper, and sorrows unfold,
In the labyrinth of streets, so old,
Lies the anguish of a story bold.
Limited by walls, confined by fate,
Gazans endure, they stand and wait,
For crumbs of mercy, for a fleeting date,
To break the chains of their captive state.
In the silence of the suffocating night,
Stars weep for Gaza, devoid of light,
Where mothers hush their children's fright,
From bombs that pierce the fragile night.
A canvas of despair, a tapestry of pain,
In Gaza's heart, where scars remain,
Echoes of suffering, a haunting refrain,
In the endless cycle of loss and gain.
Water tainted by the salt of tears,
A thirst unquenched, through endless years,
Where every drop a testament, it appears,
To resilience forged in the face of fears.
Healthcare but a distant dream,
In Gaza's reality, a distant gleam,
Where wounds deepen, and nightmares teem,
In the shattered remnants of a forgotten scheme.
Psyches fractured, spirits worn,
In Gaza's streets, where hope is torn,

By the specter of conflict, by the thorn,
That pierces through the fabric, forlorn.
Yet amidst the rubble, a spirit thrives,
In Gaza's heart, where hope revives,
In the steadfast gaze of those who strive,
For freedom's light, to emerge and contrive.
So let the world bear witness, let it see,
The siege of Gaza, the silent plea,
For justice to reign, for hearts to be free,
In Gaza's embrace, for eternity.
From the River to the Sea, Palestine Will Be Free
From the river to the sea, where olive branches sway,
In the land where tales of struggle echo, day by day,
Palestine, cradle of ancient sands and stories untold,
Your spirit, unyielding, your resilience, bold.
From the olive groves of Beit Jala to the shores of Gaza's sea,
Where the cries of children mingle with the waves, wild and free,
In every stone of Jerusalem, every alley of Ramallah's streets,
A symphony of resistance, echoing defeats.
In the shadow of the apartheid wall, where graffiti speaks truth,
And the scars of occupation bear witness, aged and uncouth,
In the refugee camps of Jenin, where dreams take flight,
Hope flickers like candles in the darkest of night.
From the citrus groves of Jaffa to the ancient ruins of Jericho's past,
Generations whisper stories of resilience that will last,
In the hearts of every Palestinian, beats a rhythm of defiance,
Against injustice, against oppression, against silence.
From the olive trees uprooted to make way for settlements,
To the families torn apart by checkpoints, by governments,
From the martyrs who've fallen, their names etched in the sand,
To the mothers who weep, holding their children's hand.
From the river to the sea, where history's ink is stained,

With the blood of martyrs, with the tears of the pained,
Palestine, land of prophets and poets, of steadfastness and grace,
Your struggle, our struggle, in every corner of this place.
From the refugee camps to the diaspora, united in our plea,
For justice, for freedom, for the right to be free,
From the river to the sea, where the sun sets in fiery glow,
Palestine will rise, Palestine will thrive, Palestine will know.
For in the hearts of the oppressed, lies a fire that won't be tamed,
A flame of hope, a spark of resistance, a dream that can't be framed,
From the river to the sea, with every breath we breathe,
We declare with unwavering certainty: Palestine will be free.

Palestine's Quest

In the silence, peace,
Palestine's heart beats as one,
Unity whispers.
Mountains stand steadfast,
Echoes of ancient wisdom,
Justice finds its path.
Amidst chaos' veil,
Balance seeks equilibrium,
Palestine's truth shines.
In the river's flow,
Hope's current never wavers,
Palestine's spirit.
Beneath the stars' gaze,
Palestine's essence glimmers,
Infinite and free.
Through cycles of time,
Resilience blooms eternal,
Palestine's legacy.
In the desert sands,
Wisdom's oasis beckons,
Palestine's truth sings.
Rooted in the earth,
Palestine's soul finds solace,
Unity's embrace.
In the dawn's embrace,
Promise of a new day breaks,
Palestine awakes.

Harmony's Cry: Palestine's Right to Be Free

In the desert sands,
Echoes of truth resonate,
Palestine's longing.
Silent olive trees,
Witness to ancient wisdom,
Palestine's story.
Rivers of sorrow,
Flow through valleys of despair,
Palestine's tears fall.
Mountains stand steadfast,
Guardians of sacred dreams,
Palestine's hope rises.
Sunrise of justice,
Paints the sky with hues of change,
Palestine's dawn breaks.
Whispers of freedom,
Carried by winds of wisdom,
Palestine's voice calls out.
Stars illuminate,
Pathways to liberation,
Palestine's journey.
Moonlight guides the way,
Towards a land of harmony,
Palestine's destiny.
In the heart's embrace,
Palestine finds peace at last,
Freedom's gentle song.

Echoes of Palestine

In the land of ancient sands, where olive trees grow,
    A tale of struggle and resilience, I shall bestow.
    Propalestine, a cry for justice, echoes through the air,
    A plea for peace and freedom, a burden hard to bear.
    From the river to the sea, a homeland once so grand,
    Where generations lived in harmony, hand in hand.
    But walls were built, dividing hearts and homes,
    Leaving scars of pain and longing, where hope roams.
    The sun sets on Gaza, where children's laughter fades,
    Amidst the ruins and rubble, hope still serenades.
    In the streets of Hebron and the hills of Nablus,
    A spirit of resistance, refusing to submit to unjust.
    Jerusalem, a city of shared faiths and dreams,
    Where coexistence wanes, torn apart at the seams.
    Yet in the alleys of the Old City, hope prevails,
    As voices rise, demanding justice that never fails.
    Oh, Palestine, a land of beauty and strife,
    Where the olive branch yearns for a peaceful life.
    Let us stand united, in solidarity we stand,
    For a future where justice and peace intertwine hand in hand.
    So let the world hear our plea, loud and clear,
    For an end to oppression and the shedding of tears.
    Propalestine, a sonnet of love and resilience,
    May your struggle find solace and your dreams find brilliance.

Palestine's Breath of Freedom

In the dawn's soft glow,
Whispers of freedom ignite,
Palestine's dreams flow.
Silent olive trees,
Witness to the tale untold,
Freedom's plea unfolds.
Sunset hues declare,
A right to skies unbounded,
Palestine, be free.
Gaza's children weep,
Yet their laughter rings so deep,
Injustice, a bane.
History's ink weaves,
Chapters of resilient hearts,
Palestine believes.
On desert sands, cries,
Echoes of freedom rise,
Unyielding spirits.
Occupied whispers,
Resilience in each breath,
Palestine's dance with death.
Graffiti on the walls,
Scripted hopes for liberty,
Palestine stands tall.
A mosaic path,
Leading to liberty's door,
Palestine, breathe free.

Jerusalem's Tears

In Jerusalem's ancient streets, where history breathes,
Whispers of faith mingle with olive-scented breeze.
Three faiths converge, in sacred embrace,
A tapestry of souls, a timeless space.
Muslims bow in reverence, toward the Dome's golden hue,
Where Prophet Muhammad ascended, the night journey anew.
Christians tread the Via Dolorosa's path of pain,
Where Jesus carried his cross, bearing humanity's stain.
Jews seek solace at the Wailing Wall's ancient stones,
Where Solomon's temple once stood, glory overthrown.
Three faiths, intertwined in Jerusalem's tale,
Where hopes and prayers in harmony prevail.
But beneath the surface of this holy ground,
Lies a city scarred by strife, where peace is seldom found.
In the shadow of minarets, and beneath church spires,
Echoes of conflict, fueled by earthly desires.
Jerusalem weeps, her tears mingling with the soil,
As generations pass, trapped in turmoil.
For in her ancient heart, lies the key,
To unlock the chains of enmity.
Let us heed Jerusalem's tears, let them soften our gaze,
And see beyond divisions, through love's gentle blaze.
For in this sacred city, our destinies entwine,
In unity lies our strength, in peace, our shrine.

Palestine's Freedom Song

In Gaza they stand,
    Yearning for freedom's embrace,
    Palestine's heartbeat.
    Olive branches sway,
    Whispers of freedom linger,
    Hope in every breath.
    Children's laughter fades,
    Underneath the shadows cast,
    Dreams still burn brightly.
    Rivers of sorrow,
    Flow through ancient lands once free,
    Palestine's tears weep.
    Mountains bear witness,
    To the struggle, to the pain,
    Palestine's courage.
    Stars illuminate,
    Night skies of resilience,
    Palestine's light shines.
    Voices rise in song,
    Chanting for liberty's call,
    Palestine's anthem.
    History's pages,
    Stained with struggles, with triumphs,
    Palestine's story.
    Until freedom reigns,
    Palestine's spirit endures,
    In hearts, in the stars.

Echoes of Sorrow

In Gaza's shadows, tales untold unfold,
Where pain and anguish, their stories mold.
A land embattled, where skies rain sorrow,
And each breath whispers of a grim tomorrow.
Here, beneath the weight of relentless strife,
Lies the human cost of a bitter life.
In Gaza's alleys, where children play,
Their laughter muffled by the echoes of dismay.
See the father, weary, with eyes worn thin,
His dreams shattered by the cruel din.
A home reduced to rubble, memories lost,
In the rubble, he counts the heavy cost.
His wife, once radiant, now bears the scars,
Of a heart torn apart by ceaseless wars.
In her embrace, a child's trembling form,
Seeking solace from the ceaseless storm.
The mother, a pillar amidst the debris,
Holds her family close, though the world may not see.
Each tear is a testament to strength untold,
In the face of darkness, her love takes hold.
But beyond the walls, where the world turns blind,
Their suffering fades in the depths of the mind.
As nations debate in chambers afar,
The human toll is but a distant scar.
Yet, in Gaza's heart, where resilience thrives,
Hope flickers in the midst of shattered lives.
For every soul lost to the ravages of hate,
A thousand voices rise to challenge fate.
In the eyes of the child, a spark ignites,
A flame of defiance against endless nights.

For in the rubble, amidst the despair,
Lies the spirit of a people, unbroken, aware.
Their stories echo through the annals of time,
A testament to endurance, a sacred rhyme.
For Gaza's children, though burdened with woe,
Hold the promise of a future yet to show.
So let the world bear witness to their plight,
And stand in solidarity, side by side.
For in Gaza's embrace, where darkness reigns,
The human cost is measured in silent pains.

Banners of Freedom

In Gaza they stand,
Seeking freedom's embrace strong,
Palestine's rightful land.
A child's innocent gaze,
Dreams of skies free and clear,
Injustice ablaze.
History whispers,
Echoes of struggle profound,
Palestine persists.
Bound by hope's pure thread,
Their voices rise, unafraid,
Palestine's heart bled.
Underneath the sun,
Their souls yearn to soar and run,
Freedom yet to come.
Amidst olive trees,
Echoes of resilience rise,
Palestine's decree.
In the rubble's wake,
Resilient spirits thrive,
Palestine awake.
Let their banners fly,
Palestine's call heard far and wide,
Freedom cannot die.

Ismail's Blessing

In barren lands where shadows linger long,
A tale of old, a son, a father strong.
Ismail, the child of Abraham's embrace,
In deserts vast, he found his sacred place.
Beneath the scorching sun, they journeyed far,
Father and son, led by a guiding star.
Through trials vast and tribulations deep,
Their faith unwavering, their promises to keep.
Like Ismail, the son, in ancient days,
Palestinians wander through life's winding ways.
Their homes besieged, their dreams confined,
Yet in their hearts, a flame of hope defined.
In Ismail's eyes, the desert's fiery glow,
Reflects the tears of those who suffer so.
Through sands of time, their footsteps trace,
The path of struggle, the enduring grace.
Their sacrifice, a testament profound,
In every hardship, in each holy ground.
The echo of their prayers, the whispers divine,
In Ismail's blessing, their spirits intertwine.
For in the heart of trials, they find release,
Divine intervention, a moment of peace.
As Ismail found water in the desert's span,
Palestinians find solace in Allah's plan.
So let us honor Ismail's tale untold,
As parallels with Palestine unfold.
In sacrifice and perseverance, they stand,
United by faith, guided by Allah's hand.

Spirit of Palestine

Amid olive groves,
    Palestine's heartbeats echo,
    Resilience blooms strong.
    Beneath crescent moon,
    Gaza's children dream of peace,
    Stars weep for their loss.
    Jerusalem's call,
    Whispers ancient tales of woe,
    Yearning for solace.
    In the West Bank's dusk,
    Hope flickers like candlelight,
    Promises afar.
    Aqsa's minarets,
    Sing songs of defiance bold,
    Echoes through the land.
    Underneath the sun,
    Occupied lands breathe as one,
    Freedom's silent plea.
    On ancient soil,
    Memory's tears softly flow,
    Roots cling to the earth.
    In Gaza's embrace,
    Resistance paints skies afire,
    With dreams yet unbound.
    Palestine's spirit,
    Unyielding through endless night,
    Dawn awaits its rise.

The Oasis of Medina

In Medina's heart, an oasis blooms,
Where unity thrives, dispelling gloom.
Guided by a prophet's gentle hand,
A community flourishes, across the land.
In the desert's embrace, they found their home,
A sanctuary from trials that roam.
Brothers and sisters, in faith they stand,
United by love, hand in hand.
Underneath Medina's radiant sky,
Diversity blossoms, like birds that fly.
Tribes once divided, now kin in embrace,
Bound by peace, a sacred grace.
In the footsteps of the Prophet's stride,
They build a haven, where hope resides.
Sharing burdens, joys, and tears,
Forging bonds that span the years.
From the wellsprings of Medina's care,
A lesson echoes through the air:
In solidarity, strength is found,
In unity, hearts are bound.
As the sun sets on Medina's scene,
Its legacy lingers, evergreen.
A beacon of hope for those in need,
A testament to unity's creed.
Oasis of Medina, in hearts enshrined,
Your spirit lives on, in every kind.
May your resilience, your love, your light,
Inspire Palestine's courageous fight.

Echoes of Injustice: Standing in Solidarity

In the land where olive trees whisper tales of old,
Where the ancient stones bear witness to stories untold,
There lies a people, resilient and proud,
Beneath the weight of injustice, they cry out loud.
Palestine, cradle of civilization's birth,
Where every grain of sand holds the secrets of the earth,
Yet in the shadow of history's grand design,
Lies a tale of oppression, a narrative malign.
In the streets of Gaza, where children play,
Their laughter mingles with echoes of dismay,
For in the air lingers the stench of despair,
As bombs rain down, leaving hearts laid bare.
Their homes reduced to rubble, their dreams turned to dust,
In the face of tyranny, they steadfastly trust,
That amidst the chaos, amidst the strife,
They'll reclaim their land, their right to life.
Injustice rears its ugly head,
As the powerful oppress the vulnerable, blood red,
Palestinian lives deemed lesser, their voices suppressed,
But in the face of adversity, they rise undeterred, unimpressed.
Solidarity echoes from every corner of the globe,
As hearts and minds unite, refusing to probe,
The lies and deception, the narratives spun,
To justify the atrocities, the battles never won.
From the streets of Ramallah to the halls of power,
From the refugee camps to the darkest hour,
We stand in solidarity, shoulder to shoulder,
With Palestine's sons and daughters, growing bolder.

For their struggle is our struggle, their pain our pain,
Injustice against one is injustice against all, we proclaim,
Their quest for self-determination, for freedom's call,
Is a beacon of hope, shining bright for all.
In the face of oppression, they stand tall,
Their spirits unbroken, they'll never fall,
For the flame of resistance burns deep within,
A flame that no occupation can ever dim.
So let us raise our voices, let us be heard,
For justice and freedom, let our every word,
Be a testament to the strength of the human soul,
As we stand with Palestine, our hearts whole.
Injustice will crumble, solidarity will reign,
And from the ashes of despair, hope will sustain,
For Palestine will be free, its people unchained,
In a world where justice and peace are finally attained.

The Call of Homeland

In lands where echoes whisper tales of strife,
Where hearts endure the weight of a displaced life,
A solemn call resounds, both near and far,
The Right of Return, a guiding star.
Through corridors of time, a people's plight,
In the hush of dawn and the veil of night,
Their voices rise, with unwavering might,
Seeking justice in the face of blight.
In the tapestry of nations, they hold a bond,
A story etched in history, profound and fond,
Their roots run deep, through the sands of time,
An identity resilient, a narrative sublime.
In the halls of justice, their voices plead,
For recognition, for the fundamental creed,
To reclaim what's theirs, what rightfully belongs,
Amidst the ruins of forgotten songs.
In the gaze of stars, in the quiet of dreams,
The diaspora yearns, as the moonlight gleams,
For a home that beckons, beyond the fray,
Where hope blooms eternal, come what may.
The Right of Return, a beacon of light,
Guiding souls through the darkest night,
In the corridors of history, it stands tall,
A testament to resilience, to one and all.
So let the world listen, let justice prevail,
Let compassion reign, let humanity sail,
For in the heart of every refugee's plea,
Lies the promise of tomorrow, unbound and free.

Voices from Gaza

In Gaza's streets, where silence speaks,
Children's cries, the world must seek.
Underneath the sun's cruel glare,
They bear the weight of despair.
In shattered homes and dusty lanes,
Innocent hearts feel piercing pains.
Their playgrounds are rubble, their laughter gone,
In a world where they're forced to carry on.
Beneath the bombs, their dreams take flight,
In the darkness of the endless night.
Their tiny hands hold onto hope,
In a land where it's hard to cope.
Their eyes reflect a haunting tale,
Of lives consumed by war's cruel gale.
Yet, in the midst of ashes and debris,
Their spirits rise, longing to be free.
Let their voices echo far and wide,
A plea for peace, a tear they hide.
For Gaza's children, let us stand,
With open hearts, a helping hand.
In the face of adversity, they find strength,
In the ruins, they still dream at length.
May their courage ignite the flame,
Of justice, in the world's domain.
Let us listen to their silent cries,
And see the truth behind the lies.
For in Gaza's children, we see the cost,
Of a conflict that cannot be lost.
So let us raise our voices high,
For Gaza's children, let us cry.

In unity, let us take a stand,
For peace to reign in their homeland.

Gaza's Lament

In Gaza's heart, where crimson sunsets paint the sky,
A land of contrasts, where hope and grief intertwine,
Children's laughter rings amidst the echoes of bombs,
Their innocence a beacon in the midst of strife's qualms.
Kites soar high, carrying dreams across the divide,
A symbol of resilience, in a place where hopes collide,
On shattered walls, they paint murals of freedom bold,
A defiance against oppression, a story yet untold.
In Gaza's lament, a tale of courage and despair,
Where every heartbeat echoes a silent prayer,
In the rubble, amidst chaos and tears,
Whispers of resilience erase all fears.
Amidst the rubble, a spirit unbroken,
In the face of adversity, words unspoken,
Gaza's children, warriors of the dust,
In their eyes, a future they trust.
So let Gaza's lament be heard,
A symphony of strength, in every word,
For in the midst of darkness, a light shines bright,
In Gaza's heart, hope takes flight.

Echoes of Peace

In the land where olive trees whisper tales of resilience,
I stand with unwavering defiance against violence's insistence.
I don't seek a mere pause in the chaos's symphony,
But a lasting peace that nurtures hope and harmony.
Let the cries of mothers silenced by grief be heard,
Let the wounds of the land be healed by every word.
I reject the notion of a temporary ceasefire,
For what we truly need is a world without the fire.
In the shadows of ancient walls, I plant seeds of unity,
Where love blooms amidst the ruins of enmity.
I don't want a momentary truce that fades with the night,
I yearn for a dawn where peace reigns, pure and bright.
So let us raise our voices, fierce and resolute,
For a future where hatred finds no root.
I don't want a cease fire, I demand an end to all hostilities,
In a world where peace flows like rivers, boundless and free.

From the River to the Sea

From the river to the sea, a land of ancient grace,
Palestine's heart beats strong, in every time and space.
Beneath the olive trees, whispers echo in the breeze,
Of a land that yearns for peace, where justice finds release.
From the river's winding path to the sea's eternal dance,
Palestinian voices rise, in a steadfast stance.
Through trials and tears, they've held onto their dreams,
Amidst the rocky shores, hope's gentle stream gleams.
From Gaza's sandy shores to the hills of the West Bank,
In the face of oppression, they refuse to thank.
For stolen homes and broken lives, their resilience stands tall,
In the face of adversity, they rise, they call.
From the river to the sea, let freedom's song resound,
Where dignity and rights, in every heart are found.
In the struggle for justice, their spirit cannot wane,
For Palestine's story, forever shall remain.
Let the world hear their plea, let justice finally reign,
From the river to the sea, let peace embrace again.

The Olive's Lament

In ancient groves where whispers linger still,
    Amidst the dust and shadows, silent, chill,
    Stands the olive, stoic sentinel of time,
    Bearing witness to a land scarred by crime.
    Roots entwined in earth's unfathomable embrace,
    Each gnarled limb tells a tale of grace,
    Yet, burdened by the weight of history's toll,
    The olive weeps, its sorrow taking hold.
    Once bathed in sunlight's golden embrace,
    Now shackled by chains of injustice, no solace,
    Its leaves, once green with hope and life's refrain,
    Now wilt beneath oppression's relentless strain.
    Oh, weary traveler of the land,
    Whose branches reach for freedom's hand,
    Your tears, like raindrops, fall upon the soil,
    Nourishing the spirit of resistance, steadfast and loyal.
    Through centuries of conquest, you've stood tall,
    Your strength a testament to the hearts that call,
    For justice, for peace, for the right to thrive,
    In the shadows of oppression, you strive.
    Though scars mar your trunk, and wounds run deep,
    Your spirit endures, steadfast, asleep,
    In the heart of every Palestinian soul,
    The olive's lament, a symphony untold.
    So let your roots anchor hope in the earth,
    Let your branches stretch towards rebirth,
    For in your resilience, we find our own,
    In the olive's lament, our courage is sown.

Morning Brews and Memories

In kitchens draped with morning light,
Where shadows dance in soft delight,
The scent of coffee fills the air,
A fragrance rich, beyond compare.
With steady hands, the pot we fill,
Grounds swirl as time stands still,
Each measured scoop, each careful pour,
Echoes of tradition, strong and sure.
In these hushed moments, memories rise,
Of days beneath unforgiving skies,
Of voices raised in songs of strife,
Of hearts that beat for a land's life.
With each swirl of the steaming brew,
We weave tales old, both tried and true,
Of ancestors who dared to dream,
Amidst the tumult's raging stream.
In these simple acts, stories are told,
Of resilience in days of old,
Of strength drawn from the earth's deep core,
Of hope that thrives forevermore.
So let the morning sun's golden gleam,
Illuminate this timeless scene,
Where coffee brews and memories blend,
In Palestinian homes, where love transcends.

Gaza Skyline

In Gaza's heart, where skies are streaked with strife,
The skyline tells a tale of endless strife.
Where towering minarets pierce the azure blue,
And shadows cast by rubble speak of what we knew.
Here, amidst the echoes of bombs that still resound,
The skyline stands, a testament profound.
A tapestry of tales etched in shattered glass,
Whispers of resilience amidst the broken mass.
In every crumbled corner, hope takes flight,
In every scarred facade, a glimmering light.
For Gaza's sons and daughters, undeterred they stand,
Defying despair with each resilient hand.
Beneath the canopy of smoke and dust,
Lies a people whose faith will never rust.
They build anew from ruins of the past,
Their spirit unbroken, their resolve steadfast.
The skyline bears witness to their steadfast grace,
A symbol of endurance in this troubled place.
For though the world may turn a blind eye,
Gaza's spirit soars, reaching heights that defy.
So let the world behold this skyline true,
A testament to the resilience we pursue.
In Gaza's heart, where hope and rubble meet,
The skyline stands, a symbol of defeat's defeat.

The Key

In twilight's hush, where shadows sigh,
    A key rests silent, under the starry sky.
    Its metal worn, its edges soft,
    A relic held, a memory aloft.
    Once, it turned with a resolute hand,
    Unlocking doors to a promised land.
    Through olive groves and jasmine's bloom,
    It whispered tales of home's perfume.
    But now it lies in quiet repose,
    A silent witness to the sorrows it knows.
    Forced from hearth and haven dear,
    Its owners scattered; their cries austere.
    Yet in its curves, a story sings,
    Of generations bound by resilient strings.
    For though they wander, far and wide,
    Their heartstrings tethered to their side.
    Oh, key of oak, with secrets kept,
    In your grooves, a legacy swept.
    With each gentle touch, a prayer is spoken,
    For the day when chains are finally broken.
    In dreams, they see their ancestral lands,
    Where olive branches brush their hands.
    And through the haze of exile's plight,
    They march towards the dawning light.
    So, let it rest, this key of old,
    A symbol of stories forever told.
    For in its grasp, hope's flame burns bright,
    Guiding home those lost in night.

Kufiyah Dreams

In every fold, a story told,
    The kufiyah whispers tales of old,
    Wrapped around with pride and grace,
    A symbol of a resilient race.
    In colors bold, like desert sands,
    It weaves through time, through distant lands,
    A testament to struggles faced,
    Yet steadfastly, its spirit embraced.
    In the breeze, it dances free,
    A flag of hope for all to see,
    Across the valleys, over hills,
    Echoing the dreams it instills.
    Through tumult's roar and silent night,
    It stands as a beacon, shining bright,
    A bond of kinship, strong and true,
    In every stitch, a pledge anew.
    Oh, kufiyah, woven with care,
    You symbolize the love we share,
    Through trials endured, you proudly gleam,
    A timeless emblem of a dream.
    In every knot, in every thread,
    Resides the spirit of the dead,
    Their voices echo in the seams,
    Guiding us through shattered dreams.
    So let us wear you, bold and tall,
    As we rise to answer destiny's call,
    With unity, with hearts agleam,
    Kufiyah, you are our eternal dream.

Tea in the Refugee Camp

In tents that echo with memories vast,
Refugees gather, a community amassed,
Tea steams amidst shared dreams,
In the midst of chaos, a moment gleams.
With each swirl of steam, stories unfold,
Tales of resilience, of hearts bold,
In the fragrant haze, hope finds its way,
Amidst the struggles, a brighter day.
The kettle's whistle, a comforting sound,
Echoes of home in a foreign ground,
Sips of solace amidst the strife,
Binding souls in this transient life.
With each cup poured, a bond is sealed,
In tea leaves' whispers, wounds are healed,
For in this simple act, unity's found,
In the refugee camp, on sacred ground.
So let the tea brew, let stories be told,
In the ink of intifada, let truths unfold,
For in these humble moments, we rise,
In the warmth of tea, under Palestine's skies.

Lyrical Rebellion

In the streets where shadows dance,
Beneath the moon's soft, silver glance,
A symphony of voices rise,
In echoes of defiant cries.
Amidst the rubble, dust, and stone,
Where hopes and dreams are overthrown,
A melody begins to bloom,
A song of resistance breaks the gloom.
Lyrical rebellion fills the air,
Notes of courage, strong and rare,
From minaret to olive grove,
A chorus rises, steadfast, bold.
In every verse, a tale untold,
Of a people's struggle, brave and old,
In every rhythm, a heartbeat strong,
In every lyric, a call to belong.
Songs of defiance, songs of might,
Ignite the flame, fuel the fight,
Against the walls that seek to confine,
Against the chains of an unjust design.
With each refrain, a spirit soars,
Beyond the barricades, beyond closed doors,
For in these songs, the soul finds wings,
And in these melodies, freedom sings.
So let the world hear this anthem true,
Of Palestine's steadfast, resilient crew,
For in the ink of intifada, forever bound,
Lies the power of songs, profound.

The Sacrifice of Ismail

In the heart of ancient sands, where whispers rise,
A father's faith, a son's unspoken cries.
Ibrahim, revered, by a divine decree,
To sacrifice his beloved Ismail, his plea.
In the stillness of the desert's vast expanse,
A bond tested, a moment's fateful dance.
With knife in hand, and a heavy heart's call,
Ibrahim sought to answer God's call.
But as the blade hovered, poised to descend,
A voice from the heavens, a message to send.
"O Ibrahim, you've shown your devotion true,
But the sacrifice is not your son, but you."
In the hush of that moment, amidst the sand's embrace,
A testament to faith, in a sacred space.
For Ismail, spared, by the will of the divine,
A symbol of hope, in a story's design.
Yet beyond the sands, in lands torn by strife,
Another sacrifice, in the rhythm of life.
Palestinian sons and daughters, with courage untold,
Their sacrifices echo, their stories unfold.
Their land, a battleground, where struggles persist,
Where dreams are shattered, and hope may resist.
But like Ibrahim's test, their faith remains strong,
In the face of injustice, they continue to belong.
For every tear shed, for every life lost,
Their resilience endures, whatever the cost.
In the sacrifice of Ismail, they find their own,
A testament to courage, in a struggle unknown.
So let their voices rise, like a desert breeze,
In the hymn of freedom, beneath olive trees.

For in their sacrifice, in their unwavering fight,
Lies the promise of justice, in the dawn's first light.

Through the Eyes of a Poet: Palestine Unveiled

In the land where the olive trees weep,
And the ancient stones whisper secrets deep,
I walk with the weight of history's sighs,
Beneath the vast and tumultuous skies.
Here, where the sun kisses the earth so tender,
Lies a tale of struggle, of heartache, of splendor.
Through the eyes of a poet, Palestine unveils,
Her stories of courage, her dreams set sail.
In Gaza's streets, where the children play,
Amidst the rubble, they find a way,
To laugh, to dance, to defy the night,
Their innocence shining, a beacon of light.
In Ramallah's squares, where voices rise,
In songs of freedom, beneath watchful eyes,
The spirit of resistance, steadfast and strong,
Echoes through alleyways, a defiant song.
In Bethlehem's fields, where the olive trees stand,
Guardians of peace in a war-torn land,
Their roots run deep, in ancestral soil,
Witnesses to sorrow, yet still they toil.
Through checkpoints and barriers, walls that divide,
Palestinian hearts beat with unwavering pride.
For in every stone, in every grain of sand,
Lies the spirit of a people who still stand.
So let the world hear our stories told,
Through the eyes of a poet, bold and bold.
For Palestine, unveiled, in all her grace,
Is a testament to the human spirit's embrace.

Though the road is long, and the journey tough,
We walk hand in hand, with hope enough,
For through the eyes of a poet, we see,
A Palestine united, proud, and free.

Voices from the Diaspora

In distant lands, our voices rise,
Echoes of a homeland's cries,
Through streets of exile, hearts entwined,
Palestinian souls, resilient, refined.
From refugee camps to city streets,
Our stories woven, our struggles meet,
In scattered lands, we forge our way,
Yet Palestine in our hearts holds sway.
In every corner, a tale to tell,
Of heritage cherished, and dreams that swell,
From generation to generation, we pass the flame,
The fire of resilience, the pride of our name.
In bustling cities, we find our place,
But never forgetting our ancestral space,
With every step, our roots still cling,
To olive groves and songs that sing.
In the diaspora, our voices blend,
A tapestry of resilience, we transcend,
The borders drawn, the seas that part,
Yet Palestine beats within each heart.
Though miles may stretch, and time may fly,
Our bond with home shall never die,
For in our veins, our homeland flows,
And in our dreams, its freedom grows.
So let our voices, loud and clear,
Resound across the hemisphere,
For Palestine, our eternal guide,
In the diaspora, our voices stride.

In the Shadow of Settlements

In the shadow of settlements, they dwell,
Where dreams are stifled, under a somber spell.
Their homes stand firm, yet not their own,
Beneath looming towers, where seeds of discord are sown.
Amidst the olive groves, they toil and strive,
With each passing day, just trying to survive.
Their fields bear witness to histories untold,
Whispering tales of resistance, brave and bold.
They wake to the echo of bulldozers' roar,
As walls rise higher, closing off their door.
Their streets are marked by checkpoints, a daily trial,
Where dignity is questioned, mile after mile.
But in the shadow of settlements, hope's flame still burns,
In the hearts of those who refuse to yearn.
For they know their roots run deep, in this ancient land,
And their spirit cannot be tamed by an oppressor's hand.
With every sunrise, they rise anew,
In the face of adversity, their resilience is true.
They paint their days with colors of defiance and pride,
In the shadow of settlements, where hope cannot be denied.
Though the weight of injustice may seem too vast,
They hold onto hope, steadfast.
For they know that one day, the shadows will fade,
And in the light of freedom, their dreams will be remade.
In the shadow of settlements, they stand tall,
Refusing to surrender, to heed the oppressor's call.
For their story is one of courage and grace,
In the shadow of settlements, they find their rightful place.

Ink of Intifada

Streets of Gaza
    Gaza's dance
    Dance beneath the moon
    Moon's soft glance
    Glance at whispered tales
    Tales in the air
    Air of a prophet's journey
    Journey just and fair
    Fair Muhammad
    Muhammad finds fame
    Fame in ink
    Ink of a fight
    Fight's guiding light
    Light in dark hours
    Hours of Palestinian plight
    Plight etched in hearts
    Hearts through turmoil
    Turmoil and shattered parts
    Parts echoing ages
    Ages steadfast and clear
    Clear courage inspired
    Inspired, banishing fear
    Fear in every tear
    Tear on Gaza's soil
    Soil of struggle
    Struggle and noble toil
    Toil of timeless creed
    Creed of justice
    Justice, compassion's call
    Call to heed

Heed the flowing ink
Ink of Intifada's spirit
Spirit let it grow
Grow and be unbowed
Unbowed testament
Testament to resilience
Resilience in Palestine's story
Story forever endowed

Afterword:

As I reflect upon the pages of "Ink of Intifada: Poems for Palestine," I am reminded of the profound power of poetry to capture the essence of struggle, resilience, and hope. In crafting these verses, I sought to offer a glimpse into the heart of Palestine, a land marked by both the beauty of its heritage and the brutality of its occupation.

Each poem within this anthology is a testament to the resilience of the Palestinian people, who continue to endure and resist despite the injustices they face daily. Through my words, I aimed to amplify the voices of those often silenced, to shed light on the untold stories, and to evoke empathy and solidarity across borders.

Writing these poems was both an act of defiance and an expression of love—for a land scarred by conflict, for a people whose spirit remains unbroken, and for a cause rooted in justice and freedom.

As the sole poet behind this anthology, I am acutely aware of the responsibility that comes with bearing witness to the struggles of others. It is my hope that these poems serve not only as a literary endeavor but also as a call to action, urging readers to stand in solidarity with the Palestinian people and to advocate for their right to self-determination.

"Ink of Intifada" is more than just a collection of verses; it is a testament to the power of words to transcend boundaries, to ignite empathy, and to inspire change. May these poems serve as a reminder that even in the darkest of times, the human spirit persists, resilient and unwavering in its quest for justice and freedom.

With gratitude,

Ismael

Ismael S. Rodriguez Jr., also known as The Bulletproof Poet, is a talented and diverse artist, author, and poet of Puerto Rican and Filipino descent. He was born and raised in Philadelphia, PA, and now lives in Oakland Park, FL. Rodriguez has a range of interests and experiences, including serving in the U.S. Navy and being deployed during Desert Storm. Despite facing numerous challenges in his life, including schizophrenia, PTSD, substance abuse, and homelessness, Rodriguez has overcome these obstacles and has been sober for 16 years. He is also actively seeking treatment for his mental and emotional health issues. In addition to his artistic pursuits, Rodriguez is an ordained reverend and practices Grey Witchcraft, Discordianism, and ceremonial magic. His website, https://thebulletproofpoet1.godaddysites.com/home, showcases his poetry, short stories, origami, and more. You can find additional links to his work on his Linktree https://linktr.ee/bulletproofpoet